UNIFORMS OF IMPERIAL & SOVIET RUSSIA IN COLOR

UNIFORMS OF IMPERIAL & SOVIET RUSSIA IN COLOR

AS ILLUSTRATED BY HERBERT KNÖTEL, D.J.

1907-1946

ROBERT W. KENNY, JR.

Schiffer Military History
Atglen, PA

Acknowledgments

This book could not have been produced without the assistance given by Peter Harrington, Curator, and the late Thomas J. McGuirl, Military Researcher, of the Anne S.K. Brown Military Collection, John Hay Library, Brown University, Providence, Rhode Island.

The Collection also contains the hundreds of uniform albums assembled by the late Col. Frederic P. Todd, West Point Museum Curator, and close friend of Mrs. Brown. Col. Todd requested that after his death the albums, also containing the artwork he commissioned of Herbert Knötel, be added to the Brown Collection.

The author also wishes to thank Roger Bender of R. James Bender Publishing, San Jose, CA, for allowing the use of information written by Thomas J. McGuirl from his publication, *The Military Advisor*.

Sources

G.A. Chresteil, "Types & Uniforms de L'Armee Rouge Vers A Berlin En 1945", Cart Libraire, Paris, 1946

Thomas McGuirl, "The Red Army in Berlin 1945-1954 (as painted by Herbert Knötel)". *The Military Advisor*, R. James Bender Publications, Fall 1998.

German Military Dictionary, TM 30-506 War Department, 20 May 1944

Benjamin Brown, "Imperial Colours - A Reference Guide to XIX Century Military Uniforms and Equipment in English, French and German", Caltrop Limited, P.O. Box 356, Millington, MD, 21651, 2000.

Dedication

Thomas McGuirl: who had the idea, started the ball rolling, and left us much too soon.

Anita Tauber, née Knötel: who shared with us her family's archives, and whose donations greatly enriched the Anne S.K. Brown Military Collection.

Book design by Robert Biondi.

Library of Congress Catalog Number: 00-109605.

Printed in China.
ISBN: 0-7643-1320-7

We are always looking for people to write books on new and related subjects. If you have an idea for a book, please contact us at the address below.

Published by Schiffer Publishing Ltd.
4880 Lower Valley Road
Atglen, PA 19310
Phone: (610) 593-1777
FAX: (610) 593-2002
E-mail: Schifferbk@aol.com.
Visit our web site at: www.schifferbooks.com
Please write for a free catalog.
This book may be purchased from the publisher.
Please include $3.95 postage.
Try your bookstore first.

In Europe, Schiffer books are distributed by:
Bushwood Books
6 Marksbury Ave.
Kew Gardens
Surrey TW9 4JF
England
Phone: 44 (0)208 392-8585
FAX: 44 (0)208 392-9876
E-mail: Bushwd@aol.com.
Free postage in the UK. Europe: air mail at cost.
Try your bookstore first.

FOREWORD

The images in this volume are from the Anne S.K. Brown Military Collection at Brown University, Providence, Rhode Island.

The first one hundred images were commissioned by Col. Frederick P. Todd, Curator of the West Point Museum to illustrate uniforms of the Russian Army from 1907-1920.

Herbert Knötel's Berlin grouping consists of forty-five images done on the scene, and includes those contracted for by the Military Intelligence Section, G-2, Berlin command in 1945. Officially known as "Series A", they were used to educate United States and Allied military personnel on the various elements of the Soviet Army. His pay for this work ranged from dollars and cigarettes to food and clothing, all of which were in short supply at this time in Berlin and the rest of Germany.

The final fifty images were commissions by Mrs. Anne S.K. Brown, the collection's founder and friend of Herbert Knötel, and covers Russian/Soviet uniforms from 1921-1946 with emphasis on the "Cold War" era.

INTRODUCTION

The author feels the best summary of the life of Herbert Knötel was written by two of his friends and fellow uniformologists: Col. John R. Elting and Col. Frederick P. Todd. The following was originally published in the Winter, 1963 issue of *The Military Collector and Historian*, the official publication of The Company of Military Historians. Herbert Knötel was both a charter Member and a Fellow.

Herbert Knötel, 1893-1963

All students of military history – and, in particular, his fellow members of the Company of Military Historians – can only mourn the recent death of Herbert Knötel, the master painter of military costume of our day. He will not be replaced easily or soon. Above and beyond his skill as an artist, he possessed vast knowledge of military subjects. His combined talents gave him a unique international authority.

Born in 1893, Herbert Knötel came to manhood at the beginning of World War I, serving at Tannenberg as a squad leader, and taking a wound there. Subsequently commissioned, he served through the war. From it, he learned the true aspect of fighting men of many nations. Ever afterwards, his pictures held a realistic edge of dust, sweat, mud, and danger.

Herbert Knötel received his first training in military artwork from his father, the famous Richard Knötel. Through the years between the two world wars he carried forward and greatly expanded the work his father had begun. He completed his father's major work, the famous *Grosse Uniformkunde*, produced the well-known *Deutsche Uniformen* cigarette card books, and illustrated a great variety of books and papers. Like his father, his outlook was universal and international; his figures were confined to no narrow region or time. In 1936 he began publishing a new series of plates to extend the coverage of the *Grosse Uniformkunde*. About the same time, he began to take an important part in the management of the Berlin Zeughaus museum, continuing in this up to the end of World War II.

The Battle of Berlin wrecked his life's work and most of his valuable private collection. Undaunted, he turned from publishing and slowly built up a new career as an artist. He also took a leading part in reviving the "Deutsche Gesellschaft für Herreskunde" (The Company's German counterpart), in which he had been active before World War II.

Though failing health and increasing age restricted his activity during the past two or three years, his hand and mind remained steady. Watercolors he painted less than a month before his death were among his finest. And eagerness for new knowledge never slackened. To the last, new information fascinated him.

Soldiers of every nation, in every age, took shape under his fingers. These were not elegant fashion plates, drawn to merely illustrate some uniform regulation of years gone by. Instead, they were a soldier's soldier – infantrymen who knew the dragging weight of a pack and an empty belly; fussy, officious administrative personnel; cavalrymen and panzer troops with eyes alert for the first flicker of hostile movement; gay, gaudy, galloping aides-de-camp. Herbert Knötel has left his armies behind him, witnesses to his mastery as a military artist.

John R. Elting
Frederick P. Todd

THE PLATES

Cavalry Generals: Parade Dress (left); Dress (right)

Senior Adjutants in parade dress. Line infantry (left) and line cavalry (right)

Adjutants of the staff of the Guard Corps and the St. Petersburg Military District

General Adjutant

1. and 2. Guards Infantry Divisions. Left: Officer of the Preobrazhenski Guards; Right: NCO of the Semyonovski Guards

Sergeant Major, 2. Guards Rifle Battalion. 3. Guards Infantry Division

Preobrazhenski Guards Regiment. Left: Subaltern in parade dress; Right: Lt. Colonel in interim uniform (frock coat)

Ismailov Guards Regiment. Left: Drummer, parade dress; Center: Lance Corporal in walking-out dress; Right: Officer in parade dress

Pavlov Guards Regiment. Left: Field Grade Officer; Right: Lance Corporal parade dress

Guards Regiment Kexholm of the Emperor of Austria. Left: soldier, parade dress; Right: officer, parade dress winter

Guards Rifle Regiment (Nr.3), parade dress. Left: Rifleman; Right: Lt. Colonel

4 Imperial Family Guards Rifle Regiment. Left: 1st Lt. in parade uniform 1910-1914. Right: Rifleman in summer dress uniform

Parade uniform, infantry of the line 1907-1914. Left: Sergeant of Infantry Regiment Wyborg Nr.85. Right: Officer of Infantry Regiment Willmanstrom Nr.86

Parade uniform, infantry of the line. Introduced in 1913. Because of the war, it was issued to few regiments. Left: Officer Infantry Regiment 115; Right: soldier, scout, Infantry Regiment 116

Drummer, infantry of the line

3 Company of 15. Infantry Regiment, Sergeant. Infantry company pennants Nos. 1-16, left to right, top to bottom

Infantry Regiments – Sergeant (right). Upper left: Officer's collar patches

Infantry Regiments. Staff officer in undress frock coat (center)

Officer, field service, with greatcoat and Bashlik (hood); machine gunner

Field service infantry of the line c. 1907, enlisted man; officer

Infantry of the line 1914-1917, 3rd and 4thh Regiments of a division

Infantry officers, 39. Infantry Division in greatcoats. Left: Staff Captain, 155. Infantry Regiment. Right: 1st Lieutenant, 156. Infantry Regiment

Grenadier Regiments Nrs. 2, 6, and 10. Lieutenant and Grenadier in field dress, c. 1907

7. Grenadier Regiment (2. Grenadier Division). Left: Sergeant Major; Right: Grenadier in parade dress

Infantry Regiment (former naval infantry regiment). Left: One-Year Volunteer and officer in parade dress

13. Life Grenadier Regiment "Erevan." Officer and Grenadier in parade dress

2. Infantry Regiment "Sofia" (Czar Alexander III), 1910. Left: Colonel; Right: Infantryman in parade dress

5. Infantry Regiment "Kalaga." Infantrymen in shirt-blouses. Left: Lance Corporal; Center: Infantryman; Right: 1st Lieutenant 1914-1917

68. Life Infantry Regiment "Borodinski." Left: Engineer Training: enlisted man in parade dress; Right: Captain in summer uniform

Infantry Regiments Nrs. 80 and 84 in parade dress. Left: enlisted man; Right: Captain

Turkestan Rifle Regiments Nrs. 1-22. Carried canvas bags tied with string as packs. Many bow-legged men served in these regiments

1. Siberian Rifle Regiment of the Emperor: left, officer; right, enlisted

The Russian Division in France, 1917. The Division was issued with French steel helmets with the Russian double eagle

Chevalier Guard Regiment. Subaltern - Lieutenant - Parade

"Horse Guards" Cavalry Regiment Staff Officer. Officer - Gala

Left to right: Life Guard, Cuirassier, Regimental Officer's. Parade - Interim - Gala

Life Guard, Cuirassier Regimental Officer's 1910-1914. Parade

Life Guard, Cuirassier Regiment of the Empress. General - overcoat. Cavalry Captain - Service

Life Guard, Cossack Regiment of the Emperor. Cossack - Parade Cavalry Captain - Gala

Life Guard, Ataman Cossack Regiment. Officer and Cossack - Parade

Left to right: Life Guard, Horse Grenadier Regiment. Officer's 1914. Service - Gala - Parade - Interim

Life Guard, Grenadier Trumpeter. Overcoat - Parade. Technical Sergeant Cavalry - Parade

Life Guard, Dragoon Regiment. Officer - Parade

Life Guard, Ulan Regiment of the Empress. Parade

Life Guard, Ulan Regiment of the Emperor. Cavalry Captain - parade. Lieutenant Colonel - Interim

Life Guard, Hussar Regiment of the Emperor. 1910. Officer's Parade Interim - Winter

Life Guard, Hussar Regiment of the Emperor. First Sergeant - Parade. Hussar Parade

Life Guard, Gnodno Hussar Regiment. Hussar - Service Dress. Technical Sergeant - Parade

Life Guard, Gnodno Hussar Regiment, 1914-1917. 1st Lieutenant Hussar Field Service

Life Guard Combined Cossack Regiment. L-R: Lieutenant Colonel, Overcoat; 1st Lieutenant, Service Dress; Lieutenant - Parade

Life Guard, Cossack Regiments. Uniform Combinations

Life Guard, Cossack Sergeant of the Semiratchenok Detachment

His Majesty's Own Life Guard, Conroy. Cossack in full dress 1907-1914

Escort to the Czar. Officer, Field Dress, Cossack Summer Uniform 1907-1914

Life Guard, Field Gendarmerie Squadron. L-R: Officer - Gala Officer - Interim Gendarm - Parade

1st Life Dragoon Regiment, Moscow. Sergeant and Officer - Dress

2nd Life Dragoon Regiment, Pskov. Dragoon in mantel (overcoat). Dragoon - Parade

4th Novotroizk Dragoon Regiment. Officer - Parade Interim - (mantel)

10th Dragoon Regiment, Novogorod. Officer - Parade. Technical Sergeant - Parade

11th Dragoon Regiment, Riga. Subaltern Parade. Lieutenant - Interim

13th Dragoon Regiment, Military Order. Subaltern & Trumpeter - Parade

14th Dragoon Regiment, Malorossky. Officer - Winter Parade - Officer - Half Fur riding uniform

17th Dragoon Regiment, Nizegorod. Sergeant Major of the Czar - Parade - Mantel

17th Dragoon Regiment, Nizegorod. Staff Officer - Parade. Officer - Interim

16th and 18th Dragoon Regiment, Seversk. 16th Dragoon Officer - Parade. 18th Dragoon Trooper - Parade

19th Dragoon Regiment Archangel. Officer's Parade Mantle and Service Cloak

Primorsk Dragoon Regiment. Officer - Parade. Sergeant - Service Dress

4th Ulan Regiment, Charkov. Technical Sergeant - Service Dress, Volunteer - Winter Parade

5th Ulan Regiment, Lithuania. Trumpeter and Staff Officer - Parade

14th Ulan Regiment, Yamburg. Captain Service and Parade

1st Hussar Regiment, Sumy. Winter Service & Dress

2nd Life Hussar Regiment, Pavlograd. Officer - Interim Hussar - Parade

5th Hussar Regiment, Alexandria. Officer - Interim Hussar - Parade

8th Hussar Regiment, Lubry. Officer and Hussar - Parade

11th Isjum Hussar Regiment. Hussar Parade 1910, Parade 1912

12th Hussar Regiment, Achtirka. Hussar - walking out Dress, Officer - Service

15th Hussar Regiment, Ukraine, 1910-1914. Left to right: General - Regimental Parade; Officer - Parade; Colonel - walking-out mantel

Crimean Cavalry Regiment of the Empress - Parade

Daghestan Cavalry Regiment - Officer 1910 Parade mantel

Turkoman Cavalry Half Regiments Officers

Don Cossack Regiments - Officer and Cossack

Orenburg Cossacks, Officers: Left: barracks dress; Right: parade dress, c. 1907

Astrachan Cossack, Trooper. Cossack cavalry traditionally wore no spurs

Asiatic Cossacks; Ussuri Cossack, left, parade uniform; Transbaikal Cossack, right, field uniform

Terek Cossacks Regiments – Trooper and Officer

1. Life Guards – Artillery brigade. 2nd Lieutenant of the 1. Battery; Right Corporal

Life Guards Heavy Howitzer or Mortar Battalion: Private and 1st Lieutenant

Guards Horse Artillery. Corporal (left) and officer (right) parade dress

Guards Don Cossack Battery, 6. Battery of the Guards Horse Artillery Regiment. Shabraque in use until 1910

Line Artillery. Regimental Adjutant, left; General, right

Line, Field and Fortress Artillery; gunner, winter uniform, left, gunner, summer uniform, right

Mounted batteries. Officer, left, gunner, right. Horse artillerymen had rifles or carbines

Mounted batteries of the Kuban and Terek Cossacks, field uniforms 1914-1918, Officer, left; gunner, right

Sapper (Engineer) Battalions, 1914-1917; Sapper, left; Officer, right

1. Caucasion Engineer Battalion, parade dress

Train. Officer, left; soldier, right, in service uniform c. 1907

Corps de Pages – Corps of Pages, left: Gala; right: Parade

Demonstration Squadron – Officer in normal winter parade dress; Trooper in parade

Gendarmerie: Officer and Sergeant of Cavalry

Corps of Border Guards – Enlisted man in parade dress; Officer in service dress

Soviet troop. General Uniform, 1917-1920

Soviet cavalry, General Uniform, 1920

Soviet infantry, General Uniform, 1920

Berlin, May 1945

Sergeant of Infantry and Private of Artillery or Armor

Air Force Major in overcoat with dress shoulder boards; Artillery Lieutenant in dress uniform with Infantry Lieutenant in same

Private & Private First Class in Summer dress uniforms

Private First Class of Military Police, Berlin 1945

Master Sergeant and Private, Berlin 1945

Senior Sergeant, Infantry and Junior Sergeant, Armor - Walking Out Dress

Lt. Colonel, Air Force Winter Dress

Lt. Colonel in overcoat, 1945

Medical Officer of an infantry regiment

Private First Class in summer uniform

Private of infantry in summer dress

Private of infantry in summer dress

Military Policeman, Berlin 1945

Privates of infantry in summer dress

Private of infantry in summer dress

Master Sergeant in summer dress

Senior 1st Lieutenant in summer dress

Major in summer dress

Senior Sergeant, tank regiment

Junior Sergeant, tank regiment

Officer of a Terek Cossack regiment

Senior Lieutenant of Artillery

Lieutenant of Artillery

1st Lieutenant, Medical Service

Lieutenant - technician - Military Police

Air Force Private, summer dress

Air Force Private, summer dress

Air Force Sergeant in mantel

Air Force 2nd Lieutenant

Captain of Artillery in summer dress uniform

Technical Service Officer of an Artillery Regiment

Sergeant First Class of Artillery in summer dress uniform

Private of Artillery in summer dress uniform

Private First Class of technical services

Private First Class of technical services

Private First Class and Private of Engineers

Chief Petty Officer - unidentified unit

Seaman in winter dress and mantel

Seaman in summer services uniform

Political Commissar of the Infantry, 1921

Cavalry - Winter uniform, 1924

Engineer Private, 1932

Corporal of Infantry, 1933

Lieutenant of Infantry, 1935-1938

Infantry - Winter uniform, 1941-1942

Infantryman in four pocket tunic called "French" after British officer who designed it

Winter uniform worn in deep cold

Paratrooper - Airborne, 1942

Lance Corporal of Infantry, 1936-1943

Lieutenant General, 1938-1943

Colonel of Artillery, 1938-1943

Flying Troops Senior Sergeant Technical Personnel, 1938-1943

2nd Lieutenant Air Maintenance Group, 1943-1945

Infantry - Winter Uniform, 1943-1945

Cavalry - Winter Uniform, 1944

Major General of Tank Troops, 1945

Sergeant of Tank Troops, 1943-1945

Tanker, 1943-1945

"Attention." Traffic Control Regulator, 1945

Commando Troop, May 1945. This man stole Herbert Knötel's and his wife's wristwatches in Berlin

Junior Medical Officer, 1945

Captain of Polish Infantry in Soviet Service, 1945

Mortar crewman with light mortar

Lance Corporal of Engineers in wading equipment, 1945

Captain of Cavalry, 1945

Captain of Cossack Cavalry, 1945

Woman auxiliary, July 1945

Infantryman, 1945

Veterinary Service, 1945

Captain State Security Service - NKVD, 1945

Lt. Colonel Veterinary Service Grand-or-Gala Uniform, 1943

General of the Air Force, 1945

Sergeant First Class State Security - KNUD - in home service dress, 1945

Colonel of Signal Troops, 1945

Don Cossacks, 1945

Don Cossacks in mantel, 1945

Lieutenant of the Kuban Cossacks, 1945 - winter

General of the Infantry Parade Dress, 1945

Captain of Infantry, 1945

Lieutenant of Infantry Parade Dress

Infantry Officers in Greatcoats

Infantryman, 1945

Corporal of the Guards Artillery, 1945

Sapper-Engineer-Corporal, 1945

Seaman, 1945

Naval Auxiliary, 1945

Actress from touring theater group Berlin, 1946

Brigadier General, Parade Dress, 1945

Air Force: Lieutenant Female Technical Services, 1946